WHAT BOOKS PRESS

AN IMPRINT OF

THE GLASS TABLE

COLLECTIVE

LOS ANGELES

ALSO BY MOLLY BENDALL AND GAIL WRONSKY

Calamity and Belle
Dear Calamity… Love, Belle

BLING & FRINGE
(THE L.A. POEMS)

MOLLY BENDALL
GAIL WRONSKY

LOS ANGELES

Copyright © 2009 by Molly Bendall and Gail Wronsky. All rights reserved. Published in the United States by What Books Press, the imprint of the Glass Table Collective, Los Angeles.

Poems from this collection have appeared in the following journals: *Colorado Review*, *Lafovea*, and *Laurel Review*.

Publisher's Cataloging-In-Publication Data

Bendall, Molly, 1961-
  Bling & fringe : (the L.A. poems) / Molly Bendall, Gail Wronsky.

  p. ; cm.

  Poems from this collection have previously appeared in the following journals: Colorado review, Lafovea and Laurel review.
  ISBN: 978-0-9823542-1-6

1. Experimental poetry, American. 2. Los Angeles (Calif.)--Poetry. 3. Fashion--Poetry. I. Wronsky, Gail Friemuth. II. Title. III. Title: Bling and fringe

PS3552.E5384 B55 2009
811./54   2009924548

What Books Press
23371 Mulholland Drive, no. 118
Los Angeles, CA 91364

WHATBOOKSPRESS.COM

Cover art: Gronk, *untitled*, mixed media on paper, 2009
Book design by Ashlee Goodwin, Fleuron Press.

BLING & FRINGE

(THE L.A. POEMS)

for Marlena Rosenthal and Vivienne St. John

CONTENTS

Preface	
Leaves/Tongues	13
Rem(ember) Me	14
Holes/My Heart	15
He's/Has Worn Out	16
Rain/Wine/Soul Music	17
New Move, Florals	18
Eyes/Fish Scales	19
Purse Between Us	20
Leaves/New Year	21
Get the Inspectors	22
Rain/The Image	23
More Clothes to Clean	24
Leaves/Influence	25
Crystal on a Rope	26
Eyes/*Faux* Leopard	27
(Blaze)er/Neo-Classic	28
Leaves/Fresh Cream	29
Casual Shoes	30
Eyes/Sincerity	31
Her Valor/Velour	32
Rain/Body Parts	33

Wafting Scents	34
Rain/This Fever	35
Circus/The Looking Glass	36
Holes/Separation Anxiety	37
Tel Quel/Telephone	38
Rain/It Raineth	39
My Hat, Interrupted	40
Holes/Tubes	41
This Season's Line	42
Holes/Fillings	43
Shadow of a Skeleton	44
Holes/Windows	45
Tokyo, My Poodle	46
Stars/Knots	47
Don't Ask/New Scarf	48

PREFACE

WE WROTE THESE POEMS "without pretensions to a romantic absolute" (Tristan Tzara). "Nowhere is there a pipe" (Michel Foucault). And of course, "even in the rain they cut the hay…which after all they did not" (Gertrude Stein). We hope you enjoy them.

MB
GW

LEAVES/TONGUES

Let   me   be   "straight"
        with you
     where   I'm coming   from:
 a word-   like   Orphic   wind-egg
(to   sigh   to wink   to   nod   to   kneel
to   shake   my   stumps   at   heaven)
         I'm   so   sure
   it's a   Notorious   B.I.G.   deal
        so what/bimbo
    I   saw   your   little   mouth-thing
now I'm   swayin
            Get
     a life   a   Sybil-leaf   a   tulle-box
by still practice   learn to
           know   my
    m(out)h   Watch   "dawn"
slink   down
     this   catwalk   wearing
     l'air du temps

REM(EMBER) ME

cellular (mole)cular
dig to that qu(ick)

back to DNA DKNY straight, easy,
clas(sic)
needs more memory

I've stored it my space with ring

tones in one
&in the nose, lip, brow

extend your self/hair

Romance it my C(hem)ical
essence

one c(elle)d

(dig)(it)al
it girl
her core
strength
the tone
gyro(tonic)
guy with tunic
fri(ends) with
w or x
toning gel
Is that Gr(eek)?
f(rag)ment

HOLES/MY HEART

      (So)litaire/(so)litude   so(lip)sism
          I   vant to be
        Brigitte Artaud   so . . . UFO-me
PLEASE   (how so?)   (how so-so)
How   (me)diocre
             but: "That's amore"
     flat abs/alien abduction
no   one   here   but us (imp)licit
     (ab)(so)(lutes)
   lover-boy
 us   WANT-ads
  (Oh night   draw   thy curtain)
    Thus: if   you   like
her   more than   you like
      me   I'll
(sew, myself!)   shut
    I'm so
        over it

HE'S/HAS WORN OUT

vintage
approximations thinning

thread-bare empirically so
tree-gone and desolate

Left Bank
frayed edge may encounter

a run or nylon ep(hem)era

selvage/salvage
file then his nar(rat)ive

(cash)(mere)
mothy
discard
distortion
salvation
army
I'm
broke
bohème
lounge
cigarette
hole

RAIN/WINE/SOUL MUSIC

"Very forward in the mouth"
if not married with caribou steak But it ought to
   age well it has: certain plum nuances
a Bur(gun)dian *vin du pays* for the (real)m
   take
      the incom(parable) Aaron N(evil)le
from the (hum)idor some *(fin) de siecle*
                                    ab(sin)the
whatever honors us:
            our bodies/our shelves the Emotions
(you just have to decide) I'm a Pussycat Doll girl
         avec Veuve Cliquot all those ska bands
from the late 70s Lady Mar(*malade*) I'm
   "dying to evolve" you're "refined
and debutante-like" I'm so sober now
       I can sing anyone
   under the p(age) or under the t(able)
don't stop in the name of love
      Go for: the big creamy finish

NEW MOVE, FLORALS

          a happening
                   that acupuncture punk
                            when all's abloom
     asanas are askew

             funereal really   (pet)als
        a mannerism   field of   poses
                    posey   pro(so)dy

       disembodied   a mere negation   with sparks
              c(lip)ped   nip it in the

                  gardening g(loves)

                    di(vine) station
                    im(pin)ge
                    sense-realm
                    summon
                    b(loss)om
                    mon jardin
                    new seeds
                    d(ashes)
                    polka dot
                    pricks

EYES/FISH SCALES

Rainbow   Rainbow   Rainbow
    like the   wo(man)   said   letting it
go   But   my   (bi)polarness
    cast its   line   too
far   this   time
   and   all the   dew-drops   in the Leaves
     of Gr(ass)   are   rolling   their eyeballs
I'm in a   working-class
    neighborhood   gallery/   coffee house/
perfor(man)ce space/   micro-   brewery
    full of   cultural terrorists
         so
Doom me
      I mean   Un-   Doom   me
I   died   for   you   on the   (opera)ting
  table my   fish-   tail   jerking and
twinkling   What   an   out-of-body
    moment

PURSE BETWEEN US

```
    surplus
                even if disp(lace)d
 accessory to        (bar)riers
            secrets

         pur(pose)ful    mother's
    make up          powder/power

          lost/hidden         loss
       harder than to master

         (Wear it!)    on your shoulder
```

excess/access
pull
dual
d(raw)string
egg sac
sea life
(tote)mic
bags
carry on
presence/absence

LEAVES/NEW YEAR

      Me   and   James Dean   are   "sexy"
my dog is   "a good friend"   my
    sister-in-law   "the   tree   of   self-im(posed)
chastity"   Have some   Chinese
     Astrology   tea   *oui?*   Bee-
g(odd)ess   forgive   me   Tis   the
y(ear)   of   the   poet
     (lest   we   be   forgot)
like: Lalla   jumping mad
   DON'T   MOON   ME   and
the yew tree   with   its   "insatiable appetite"
   "like death"   This is "the end
of   the   year   as well as of
      the   poem"   This
 is the new *langue* sign:
I put it on   your bar tab

GET THE INSPECTORS

      elegiac field   charged with

  a little metal ad(vice) I'd give
    mesh   chain link   belt

    refugee   exile of self
          my string theory

    thong   with negative space
less governing
         pharmaceutical charm

    enhancers inhi(biters)

check point‡ border which camp fatigued with my razor phone il(leg)al baggy pants alienated (butch)er new at target

RAIN/THE IMAGE

    E(pit)aphs
                      dust   Our paper
(the title's arbitrariness)   a   filmy   thinness
   non-place/in person   an absence
                           (as)cending
over here, over there   a pipe, a key, a leaf, a glass
    I love you: juxtaposition of   horse
  and armchair   the s(or)cery of his silhouette
                 a *revelation*
  not unlike/no two alike
                  exotic dancer   hairstyles
  the f(all)   fall fashion   after the
                   rain came
it   all   unraveled
       losing/loosening   the word as noose
a s(matter)ing of g(litter)   on the   pavement

MORE CLOTHES TO CLEAN

```
I found a            outside
   I was inside my sweater

                        unpursuable
  towardness
          gathering lint on the way home

          gathering sand on the way
self--are you?
                black turtleneck
    in the laundry

               state of turning
               state of tumbling

    that moment of--click--hesitate--
                 the buzzer
```

                       sup(posit)ion
                    deli(cat)e
                 fabric softener
               materiality
            think again
         inner/outer
      before washing
   rinse
 the afterward
indeterminate stain
re-formulate
re-versible.

LEAVES/INFLUENCE

       He said/she said: *a   noise   within*
           my   tombs/tone
(all   the   perfumes   of   Arabia
           can't   un-leash   me)
love soaked/brain soaked
                   Leggo my eggo
      Daddy-o
  I've   beat   feet   to
Little Saigon   Beats   ret(urn)ing
     in a   Nile-on   rug

   You have: *Sappho*   eyelashes
           You have: a cellophane/cellphone
in your
   brain   I (scat)ter:
  pearls   before   Swinburne
     and   after   making
   love
     I hear   *Flourish.*
Exeunt   *omnes.*

CRYSTAL ON A ROPE

                        dive in transparence
        crystal blue persuasion

                            more tales
        to live by
                        Kris Kringle/Kristeva
            my new age angel/angle

        directionality   cut glass

            critique/Lalique
        facet
                            turn it   off

                                            aftermath of
                                        culture/suture
                                    sharp
                                    razor
                                looking glass
                            stage
                            lucite
                            (bang)les
                            light up
                        sheerness
                        wear it around
                        my neck

EYES/*FAUX* LEOPARD

```
        You were              looking at me
w(hen)      my      girl-group     p(lay)ed
        Club         (Linger)ie          ce soir
we were      so           Monique       so
    (Wit)tig        in our       see-through
s(pots)        our      (Gap)       jeans
     you     per(used)    me    bad   primitivo
    s(ur)f-boy       you      duded me
deluded     me    with    your     m(I'm)e
    r(out)ine        your      Geek
         élégance       Monsieur    Medusa
s(lay)    me     I    mean     f(lay)    me
        in    y(our)    temple-tomb    lift up
mine skin       YOU ARE:     Paul de Man:
    RuPaul:            demain
                 man
```

(BLAZE)ER/NEO-CLASSIC

         black tailcoat   wet feathers
                      transmute/trans(late)
     motoring to empha(size)
                speedboat   in her wake
          tycoon   synthesis
                         smoothed & geled
          hairless   zipped up   neat   straight up
             martini lounge   Yma Sumac
     Call me princess
                                              d
                                              r
                                      t   i
                                      u   p
                                      x   h   p
                                      e   i   i
                                  y   d   s   n
                                  e   o   g
                              s   l
                              t   (s
                              i   l   t
                              n   o   a
                      s   g   w   s
                      h   h   )   h
                      a   t
                      d   n   j
                      e   e   a
                      s   s   c
                              s   k
                  i
                  n   (e
                          f   b   t
                  s   l   u   s
                  e   y   t
                  a   )
                  m   b
                          e   o
                  m   e   n
                  e   '
                  t   s   h
                  a
                  -       k   o
                  s   n   l
                  l   e   e
                  e   e
                  a   s
                  z
                  e

LEAVES/FRESH CREAM

The   Wittgenstein   home   in Vienna   held   seven   grand   pianos   five   sons   three   suicides   one   by   drowning   one   by   gunshot   one   by   poison   Don't   let   me   get   st(art)ed   on   the   mat(he)matics   of it   The   s(ham)anism   what floats   what   remains   unaccounted   for   in   the   sequined   l(edge)r   books   of the   genes

CASUAL SHOES

                    my heels=a thing of the present
     mindful/plaidful

                semi-self-aware
     more emptiness haunts and stirs

           high pitched sketchers   thy shoes
                    thy kirtle

            LIke them?   idee fixe

     Uggs, I've forgotten   How to dance

        bottom of it   shank   vamp
           so stroll   the arcade
                             with Benjamin

         he's (out)side   no,   inside

                            the reference?
                         What was
                       fluxu(ate)
                     kvetching
                   fetching
                 edgy
                marginality
                the crust
              corridor
             pro(men)ade
           unshoe him!
          non-issue oriented
         about to be

EYES/SINCERITY

```
            Mama         Paloma
Picasso   is         sincere       she
   calls me      Gertrude-ita     from a                    mouth
that             dies           I'm            married
to it         mu(chacha)        I'm        Charo-full
       in my Escada          dress          mi mantilla
verde        con halo       made of
       ojos de         (sin)ceri(dad)    What rhymes
with         duende:           nada
What    rhymes              with            carnival:
          mi casa         Write this
down:               my             black    horse
        has       black      eyes      from
(Chic)hen Itza)            yo          Sorry but
                  mañana
    isn't              good          for me
```

HER VALOR/VELOUR

Load on the velvety
        <u>chenille</u> in my cocoon

I'm waiting   for my fuzz

     to go away
             aspiring <u>papillion</u>
  ontology   to be in softness

  and bouclé   sp(lit) self
   so many selves

             metamorphosis

[The following words appear in vertical columns, read top-to-bottom, left-to-right:]

tiger(swallow)tail synthesis photo flick her Kate Moss mossy wilderness out in the cold duplicitous crawl until you drop lure velour

RAIN/BODY PARTS

    my *milagro* fetishes   here's a heart
here's a kidney   a doll's leg   Is this yo(ur) uter(us)?
  which end(')s up   the knee, the elbow, its iffigy
    ex-(is)tence again, the obscurity concerning the
vagina   But it's a (but)chery I   love
  nude pantyhose   the red apricot blossoming
your jade letter-opener sl(icing) through p(rose) I (but)ter
    my face   effacing   surfaces
and what about   eye sockets, nostrils, m(out)hs, ears,
  navels?   all (pen)etrable
    Elle hurlait son orgasme   *a la nuit*
  our m(own) p(laces)   a por(no)graphy of
         p(art)s
  morning star/porn star   an(atom)y lessons
a c(harm) bracelet ankle s(trap)   The Cure

WAFTING SCENTS

perfume/perform
your roll on   l'eau de toilette

boudoir   booty shake
scratch and sniff skin

New Historicism
my limelight
the green light glow

incense   incest   in style   (me)(moi)r

smell oriented
Orient
harem
PJ's
silk (pill)ows
smoke puffs
c(ouch) talk
opiate
bed rest
head rest
s(elf)ness

RAIN/THIS FEVER

        Catch it: mi(me)sis   or parody?
*(she   looks   like sleep/   As she would
                catch another Antony)*
    at her (toil)et
alchemizing   demon-possession   into sweat
   (yet: falling   in love   is not a   subtler
        metamorphosis)
See   the   Virtual   Giantess   On   Fire
         perish once/perish twice
   turn on (turn on!)   the virus detector
give/head/cold
      Noble   tote(mist)ic   the ill wind requires
   a corpus
spargere: to scatter   (all erotic signifiers fly)
   Un-like   her   Examiner's
  shiny   black   Armani   (medici)ne
bag: *Do drop in*   he offers
    opening its mouth   a little   wider

CIRCUS, THE LOOKING GLASS

high wire defends and shuns

contortionist   stretch tights

Hurry   look up
simultaneity

grasp   grasp
No real clown regard in her leotard/Lyotard

tent of desire/death

ring of containment
cage
tame
abandonment
demand/desire
big other
big top
makeup
bare back
stallions
performative
tied up
tight rope

HOLES/SEPARATION ANXIETY

        Call me   "unreliable"
pull apart/fall apart   the old *fort-da*
    at the airport
           You go/Godot!
  you're "autumnal"
a   gypsy girl   dragged off   by the g(end)armes
     TAKE ONE!
        it's   "subterranean"
Get a: *peignoir/bête noir/nom de plume*   life
"complicit"
     caught   red-handed   with the Louis Vuitton
   in   "tufted emerald"
  Departure/aperture
         my own bravado   murders
    the "metaphor"
        of c(losing)

TEL QUEL/TELEPHONE

      press the lb.   symbol
                         calling all girls
        Barbie phone
     talk it out   inter(vent)ion
        ear phones   muffs

  self-annihilate   auto-erotic
      Freudie, nub me with a dial tone

                               message/massage
                          busy
                      (sign)al
              sweep it under
           chassé
         seizure
       on hold
     Saussure
    inflict
  call on a (pro)noun
to undo

RAIN/IT RAINETH

      The End   of the World
whose   liquid   murmur heard
  new   thirst
          it's a witnessing   without
Mil(tonic)   over-   seeing
   40 days/40 something
           (cumulus maximus!)
I need   a   foul-weather   merry-widow
   to s(oo)the me
to assuage the   hurly-burly   Do
   the   hokey-pokey   with   the little
  tiny handprints   of the rain (quick, cummings)
Keep touching me!   D(rip) d(rape)
      your b(lack) sunshine
          all around me
D(ark) Madonna   in Hot Topic
   hood/dead   raingear: Sleep it
 off   goth-girl: thus
  e(merges)   virgin earth

MY HAT, INTERRUPTED

```
                  a beret moment
        tête à tête

           in the hood
        Hades' head of blue flames

                 Daphne's leaf hat

        soft feathered cloche      siren
                    Zeus/chartreuse
                 bouffant/buffet
                                beanie tease
                                        bubble
                                    brimming over
                                    my h(air)
                                toque/toke
                              pill box
                            crowned
                          tiara
                        top hat
                      banquet
                    pas(try)
                  (bag)uette
                headbirths
```

HOLES/TUBES

Down the:
        vein/drain with   vanity/you Manichean
  in a   hopeless/slipdress
no wonder   you're   "not getting any"
     LiPo suction
              you're   "wry"
"impassioned"   "realistic"
at   long   last: Queen of the Whole Shebang
     the   panicky   galaxy
Marry me!
               my trade-mark
  "simplicity"   and   Cupid's after-shave
will save us   there's an   A-bomb in
     my (bra)in
            worm hole/hell hole
some *pot de crème?*   I mean it:
      we used to be
   teenagers

THIS SEASON'S LINE

If it's   écrire/écru
                    crewneck & sandals

    sublimate these lime-green
                            culottes
  the seeming
        between   on the topic
                of jersey

  Ask what is left off
        swimming inside the clear

                    layers of separateness

```
                    t c b a s y s m r m n i
                    o l i b o o o a o a e n
                    p a n s f u v n v n w (
                    s s a ( t   i d i d f s
                      h r o e   n o n o r i
                      i i r n   g m g m a n
                      n s b         & m )
                      g m )         m e u
                        )           a s a
                      s f           t     t
                      h r           c     e
                      a o           h
                      d m
                      e
                      s z
                        e
                        i
                        t
                        g
                        e
                        i
                        s
                        t
```

(reading vertically: tops / clashing shades / binarism / abs(orb) shock / soften / safe from zeitgeist / you are / moving / random / mix & match / new frames / in(sin)uate)

HOLES/FILLINGS

More   night!
               More   nebulae!
In love with: "the   world's   most
    beautifully   designed   rug"

El teatro de
          you & me   and the espaliered
apricot tree
        (isn't it   digital?
indigenous?)   a   dignified/signifier
from the   land   of
      (roman)ce   novels
    and   (Myst)icism   Whisper it:
the password/   the   curse word/
    the s/word in   the   throat
  of   the   world's   most
elegant   poet:
                  More
     s(cope)
for the   t(end)er   embassy—
    more *d'eau!*

SHADOW OF A SKELETON

                  this weather hurts
    Want to see mine?

                          a little face work
          angel charm   some R(ilk)le

     Diva   devotional
a little night music

              female female impersonator
      pseudo-perversion   pre(script)ion

                  skin & spa
                           if I could rave
       in my jail-bait nailpolish
   how smoothly it goes
                    so sue me

                                    give in
                              her meetings
                            artists
                        anonymous
                      old injury
                   insure/ensure
                cover st(ick)
              foundation
            comp(act)
          secret locket
        her fraud
      re(veal)
    revel in it
  don't tell

HOLES/WINDOWS

"to   cut   a   shape   in   time"
                (the intensest curlicue) it's
the   least
                we   can   do: jump
through   hoop-earrings/fine-tuning
  f(rocks)   into   bitches

TOKYO, MY POODLE

Hello Kitty
                        and my plastic hair

    (God)zilla me Issey Miyake
                           the sound of

Sailor Moon
Who's your favorite designer?

              Sayonara

                                 B(ash)o
                                 my sign/your sign
                                 we all sign for
                                 asymmetry
                                 metallic
                                 bullet
                                 toy dog
                                 girly bubble
                                 com(mod)ification
                                 pa(god)a
                                 empire

STARS/KNOTS

Walpurgis   knot   a little   naught
    music   oh   my   ent(angle)ments
dis-cussioning   and   fistfuls   of disco dollars in
    the belly of   some Revlon-elation   I'm
all   tied   up   with   now(here) to
    self-fashion   Masseuse me
Zeus!   my hair is so tangled I can't even   kill you
    the   flower-net   of   intentionality
is   falling   out   the knots   the
    fathers   the   feminisms   ooh   sweet *fascista*

k(no)tty heaven   k(not)ty women   n(aught)y pine

DON'T ASK, NEW SCARF

```
    via his sports car
                put a soundt(rack) behind

wind-machine                    sm(ear)   blur
            superim(pose)d

    on the verge of Italian blue
            like gold to airy thinness

went for the beige

        s(wept) up                  (convert)ible
                                                a
                                              v c
                                            s i t
                                          w t r u
                                        s r a t a
                                      k i o t u l
                                    h e t n i a i
                                  ( p r u g  l t
                                c p i ( a   s i y
                              i i t c t   s t t
                            m n ) h i   t a a y
                          c a y   i o   a t t
                        a r   i   e n   t i i
                        r t   n       i o o
                        r i   (       o n n
                        y a   p       n
                          
                        o     i
                        n     n
                              )
                              k
```

MOLLY BENDALL is the author of four books of poetry, *After Estrangement*, *Dark Summer*, *Ariadne's Island*, and most recently *Under the Quick* from Parlor Press. She has also co-authored with Gail Wronsky two books of cowgirl poetry. She currently teaches at the University of Southern California.

GAIL WRONSKY is the author of three books of poetry: *Again the Gemini are in the Orchard*, *Dying for Beauty*, and *Poems for Infidels*; a novel: *The Love-talkers*; a book of translations: *Volando Bajito*, poems by Alicia Partnoy, and two books of cowgirl poetry co-authored with Molly Bendall. She is Director of Creative Writing and Syntext at Loyola Marymount University.

www.ingramcontent.com/pod-product-compliance
Lightning Source LLC
Chambersburg PA
CBHW032018290426

44109CB00013B/712